Writing   for   the   Fun   of   It

Robert C. Hawley, Ed.D.
Isabel L. Hawley, Ph.D.

WRITING

for the

FUN OF IT

An Experience-Based Approach
to Composition

E R A   Press
Education Research Associates
Amherst, Massachusetts
1974

Published by E R A Press
Education Research Associates
Box 767
Amherst, Massachusetts

ISBN 0-913636-02-9

*Library of Congress Catalog Card Number
73-83548*

Manufactured in the United States of America

FOREWORD

This book is based on the premise that the teaching of composition need not and should not be the drudgery for both teacher and student that it often is. Properly approached, writing, learning, and learning to write are fun. It is our hope that the students who participate in the activities in this book will discover the fun in writing as they sharpen their communication skills, and that the teachers who use the approach advocated here will find their experience both enjoyable and rewarding.

As a form of self-expression, writing needs all of the things the self needs—acceptance, constructive feedback, nourishment, and the caring society of others. The student needs assurance that when he puts a part of himself into a piece of writing, his writing *will be read* by an audience that cares about both him and his writing. To enjoy writing, the writer must know that his work will be accepted on its own terms and not be subjected against his will or without his knowledge to judgment either against external standards of perfection or in competition with the writing of others.

These needs are best fulfilled in a

classroom in which students and teacher
know and trust one another and work coop-
eratively to achieve the goals of the class.
In such a classroom students help one another, collaborate when appropriate, and
support one another's efforts rather than
each student competing against all the rest
for the highest grade. Such evaluation as
is desirable or necessary is done on a mu-
tually agreed-upon basis.

Without doubt the largest single consideration which prevents people from en-
joying writing is the fear that their writing will be judged (negatively) on the basis
of the way it is expressed rather than received as a message being communicated,
whether well or badly. Correctness and
effectiveness of expression are, of course,
proper subjects for study—but *after* the
need for them has been established through
the production of significant writing. With
this principle in mind, we have concerned
ourselves in this book with generating ideas
and materials and providing opportunities
for writing. Revising and polishing can be
done only after the major content and structure of the composition are in concrete form.

We wish to express our gratitude to all
the teachers who have tried out activities
included in this book and provided us with
valuable feedback. And we thank especially
the many students who have, wittingly or un-
wittingly, participated in the evolution of
the approach to teaching writing described
in this book and the development of the activities included here.

CONTENTS

I:

TEACHING WRITING

Chapter 1:

WHAT MAKES WRITING FUN

How many personal letters do you have on your mind to write? One? Five? Seven? Why is it that you haven't written them yet? If you're anything like us, chances are that you have several letters of obligation outstanding, along with some others that you really ought to write. And although we can complain that we just haven't had the time to write them, we suspect that the real reason for putting them off is that we somehow dread the thought of putting pen to paper and starting to write. But what could be a more pleasant task, ostensibly, than communicating with a friend? Why is it that the act of writing seems to put so many of us off?

Our guess is that this is an attitude we learned in school: Writing is difficult. It's hard work. There are so many things you have to watch for—spelling, punctua-

tion, correct usage. It's hard to say what
you really mean. You've got to go over it
carefully, and still the teacher will find
something wrong. In fact, as Ken Kesey has
pointed out, when we sit down to write, many
of us have the feeling that the teacher is
standing there by our shoulder, just waiting to mark up our paper with a big red
pencil.

Technical competence in writing, such
as that demonstrated for the writing sample
in the College Board exam, often comes at a
very high cost in terms of attitude toward
writing. And technical competence in writing is often achieved only by the "winners"—
the *A* or *A-* or *B+* students. What happens to
the losers in the writing class? What happens to those who never really master the
semi-colon or the concept of emphasis? Those
students turn out to be double losers: They
didn't learn technical competence, and they
did learn to dislike writing, to stay away
from the act of writing whenever possible.

For the double losers, for those who
have banished writing from their repertory
of personal activities, the loss is all the
greater because they have lost writing as a
discovery tool, as a vehicle which provides
the individual with an opportunity to clarify his own thinking and feeling, to reflect
upon his acting, and to test his power over
his environment. Even the winners often
come away from the writing class with the
feeling that writing is hard work and not
very much fun.

But good writing, clear writing, *is* hard work—everyone knows that. Why should we try to make it fun? The answer is because fun is a motivator for hard work, as anyone who has played three sets of tennis on a hot day can tell you. True, we can work hard and not have fun. Yet when the work is meaningful, when it touches our lives in a significant way, when we find in it a joy of discovering new power, then our hard work—whatever it may be—can be fun.

The reason for making writing fun for students is not to seduce them into accomplishing an essentially odious task. We are not advocating sugar-coated medicine. Rather we are attempting to help students find writing as a useful tool for themselves, a tool of self-expression, of communication, of discovery and power—and thus a self-fulfilling, joyful task.

What makes writing fun? What makes writing *not* fun? If we can determine the conditions that make writing fun and not fun, then perhaps we can plan writing lessons to take these conditions into account. Nothing is absolute, however, and the conditions that make writing fun in one setting may make it not fun in another. We have listed below conditions that we feel often determine whether writing is fun or not.

What Makes Writing NOT Fun:

—The feeling that you can't win (in competition with others in the class or with

the teacher, who always knows best).
—Anticipation of negative evaluation.
—A feeling that the subject is unimportant.
—Anticipation of an insufficient or unin-
terested, uncaring audience.
—Fear that the piece of writing won't be
read, used, or published.
—Anticipation of unfavorable comparison to
the work of others.
—Anticipation of unfavorable comparison to
the work of professionals.
—Anticipation of nit-picking criticism
which ignores the larger message.
—Anticipation that the work will be mis-
understood by an unperceptive or uncaring
audience.
—Fear that the audience will focus on what
you think is minor, unimportant.
—Inadequate information.
—Inadequate physical equipment—pen, pencil,
paper, typewriter.
—Time pressure, with evaluation that ignores the lack of time.
—Pressure for perfection without regard
to time—"Take all the time you need, just
get it perfect."
—Unrealistic view of the student's available time.
—Distractions—other, more pressing inter-
ests.
—Memory of previous unsuccessful efforts.
—Memories of past unpleasantnesses connected with attempts at writing.
—The fear that you will be locked in and
held accountable forever for what you com-
mit to writing.

What Makes Writing Fun:

—Discovering new things about your subject.
—Discovering new things about yourself.
—Discovering that you have more creativity than you formerly believed.
—Anticipation that someone will read your work and be moved, pleased, delighted, amused, appreciative.
—Anticipation of exercising control or influence over another person.
—Making a good work.
—Creating something useful.
—Making a beautiful work.
—Stating a truth.
—Creating a monument to oneself.
—Creating a tribute to a loved one.
—Spreading the word about something you care about.
—Recording thoughts in a permanent form.
—Anticipating praise for a job well done.
—Anticipating self-respect for the finished product.

These lists are tentative, provided in the spirit of brainstorming. You may wish to make additions and deletions, elaborate on some points, or flatly reject some. Use this catalogue as a sounding board for your own thinking.

Chapter 2:

"MY SUMMER VACATION"—
GATHERING, ORGANIZING, & PRESENTING
INFORMATION

What's wrong with "My Summer Vacation" as a composition topic? The students have been away all summer and have had hour upon hour of non-school experience to write a-bout. Yet invariably when we assigned such a topic to our returning students, there would be moans and general complaints, and someone would be sure to say, "I've tried to think, but I really didn't do *anything* during my summer vacation."

This situation is at least in part due to the fact that as the student takes out a blank sheet of paper and places the pencil point at the left-hand side of the top line, he or she looks back over a seemingly endless chain of undistinguish-able, undifferentiated time, looks forward over the blank sheet of paper, and con-cludes that there is no way to get the two together.

This student is defeated because he or she is trying to perform three separate critical thinking functions at the same

time—gathering, organizing, and presenting the information. Examine what this
student is attempting: He is trying to
recall the events that took place over the
course of two or three months. Simultaneously he is trying to *organize* those
events in some meaningful fashion. And
at the same time he is trying to *present*
those organized events in a mode and style
that will be understandable and interesting to the intended audience. The student
is stuck with a blank piece of paper because he has an unclear notion about what
function he is performing. By trying to
do the three functions at the same time,
the student is unable to do any of them.

Now let's lead the student through
the three functions, one at a time: First,
generate the information—brainstorm for
three minutes all the things that you did
during your summer vacation—work for as
long a list as possible, put down anything
that comes into your head—don't screen
the list—even the zany, way-out ideas.
(For the rules of brainstorming, see pages 9-
10 below.) Second, organize the raw data—
search for patterns, combine similar items,
compare, contrast, cross out unimportant
items, circle very important ones, rank-
order your list. And finally, present your
organized information—determine what is
the best vehicle, considering your intended audience: poem, play, essay, story,
movie, videotape, comic book, newspaper,
letter. If your teacher has specified the
type of writing to use for presentation,

then consider how your organized information can best fit that assignment.

   If the student takes these three steps
in order, chances are that he will find
that there is far too much to say, rather
than too little, and the task will be to
pare down the work to the size of the intended assignment. Let's examine these
three critical and creative thinking functions:

GATHERING INFORMATION:
   The first step is gathering data—collecting, generating, making up, devising,
pulling together, inventing, amassing items
which may later prove to be useful. This
collection forms the raw material from
which the finished product is made. Nat-
urally, the richer this collection is with
specific detail, variety, and unique items,
the more likely that the finished product
will be a rich and successful piece of
writing. The student writer too often
works from a very small base of information, and thus it seems that there really
isn't very much to write about. On the
other hand, when the writer has amassed a
large body of raw material from which to
draw his piece, then the problem becomes
quite different: Now the problem is to
select and organize, pare down that great
bulk of raw material so that it can become a meaningful piece of writing for a
particular audience. The problem has
changed from trying to think of something

to say to one of deciding what *not* to say.

Perhaps the single most important technique for gathering data is brainstorming. Brainstorming is a structured method of increasing the flow of ideas and tapping into an often unused stream of creativity for both groups and individuals. The rules of brainstorming are designed specifically to decrease the anxiety that often accompanies the search for new ideas; thus it raises the level of personal energy available to work on generating ideas.

Brainstorming can be taught as a skill, and teachers who have taught their classes to brainstorm are often amazed at the increased level of creative thinking which the technique helps to provide. The rules should be posted on a large poster for all to see:

1. No negative evaluation during the brainstorming period. (No one says, *"Well, the trouble with that ideas is . . ."* or *"Well, that isn't really what he asked us to brainstorm about, was it?"* Every idea is accepted at face value.)

2. Work for quantity. (The longer the list of items the better. Later there will be time to sort out and eliminate, but during the brainstorming period, work for quantity, not quality.)

3. Zany, far-out ideas are encouraged. (There are no "wrong" ideas, and furthermore, the more unusual the better. A far-out and obviously unworkable idea often

triggers a new way of looking at the problem or has the germ of a useful idea within it.)

4. Springboard or piggy-back from
idea to idea. (Let one idea trigger another.)

5. Record each idea. (Note down a
key word or phrase which will remind you
about each idea. Then after the brainstorming period all the ideas can be re-
viewed.)

6. Set and keep a strict time limit.
(The realization that the brainstorming
period is limited, that the brainstormers
are working against the clock, helps to
keep a high level of personal energy throughout the period.)

When introducing brainstorming as a
skill, it's useful to start with a zany
topic such as "ways to improve the bath-
tub," or "uses for a junked car on a desert
island," or "new ways to celebrate Thanksgiving." Have the class brainstorm on one
of those topics for three or four minutes
with two or three recorders taking turns
writing the ideas on the board. Then, as
a quickie writing assignment, ask the students each to spend five minutes writing a
paragraph essay on the topic that was brainstormed, using any of the ideas from the
brainstormed list as they choose. At the
end of the five minutes the teacher can
call for volunteers to read their essays,
or better still, the class can divide into
groups of four or five, and each student

can read his essay to the others in his group.

This exercise teaches not only brainstorming, but also the way that brainstorming fits into the three-step critical thinking process. After the class has gathered information (through brainstorming), then the individuals organize that information, mainly by selecting items of interest, and present it in a short essay.

The same three-step process can be applied to writing a poem, a research paper, or a novel. The poet, researcher, or novelist who gathers his information using a brainstorming approach finds a rich deposit of raw material to shape into the final piece. While most professional poets, researchers, or novelists probably don't use formal brainstorming in their work, we suspect that they look at the world with something akin to a brainstormer's eye: The poet looks at his subject from as many angles as possible and then distills his findings into verse; the researcher gathers as much data as possible and then finds patterns of meaning in it; the novelist looks at the world around him in all its richness and variety and then shapes it into an organic whole. David D. Britton has said that the difference between an amateur writer and a professional is that the amateur looks at a blank piece of paper and wonders, "How can I possibly fill this with writing?" while the professional looks at the world and says, "How can I possibly

reduce all of this to but a few printed
pages?"

Perhaps the most important aspect of
brainstorming is the non-judgmental, non-
evaluative attitude which it fosters. Pre-
judgment closes the door to discovery and
blocks the path to creativity. New creations are almost always the result of discovering new or unusual relationships between existing things. When we see things
only in the light of their old, preexist-
ing positions and relationships, then our
chance of finding new insights or making
new discoveries is low. On the other hand,
when we allow ourselves to be fanciful, to
speculate on new possible relationships between common things, then our chances of
making discoveries, of creating something
new are considerably higher.

For example, take this exercise:
Brainstorm for four minutes ways that
a child is like a kaleidoscope. E. g.:

unexpected fun
never ending
prismatic
like jewels
individual
you can use it as a tool
one looks into them
the outside is different from the inside
from the wrong end—very dull
uninteresting if you don't know how
     to look at it
beautiful
forming beautiful patterns

elusive
glorious
delicate
bizarre
frustrating but wonderful
attention getting
aurora borealis
never there when you want it
colorful
more complex than you think
seems simple on the outside
easy to hold
breakable
fragile
multi-faceted
never quite the same
always changing
changing patterns
bright pattern of life
serendipitous
moves around a lot
. . . (twenty-two more items) . . .

Next count the syllables for each item on the list.

Now choose a five-syllable item from the list to be the first line of your haiku. You may combine items such as a two-syllable and a three-syllable item to make this first line. Then search for a seven-syllable item from the list, again combining items if you wish. Finally, complete your haiku by finding or devising a second five-syllable line. The poem should be entitled "The Child." (Time limit, five minutes.)

The following examples were generated from the list above at a recent workshop for teachers:

> *THE CHILD*
> *Unexpected fun*
> *Forming beautiful patterns*
> *Fragile, bright, joyful.*

> *THE CHILD*
> *Multi-faceted*
> *Never there when you want it*
> *Unpredictable.*

> *THE CHILD*
> *Bright pattern of life*
> *Never ending source of joy*
> *Change without notice.*

> *THE CHILD*
> *Serendipitous*
> *Sees the world new all the time*
> *Pretty in himself.*

> *THE CHILD*
> *Indefinable*
> *Differs outside from within*
> *Burst of energy.*

Here again the three-step critical thinking process has been in use: Gathering information by brainstorming on a metaphor, organizing that information by counting syllables and choosing items which fit a specific pattern of syllable counts, and finally displaying the organized information as a poem.

This haiku activity leads us to the

second method for gathering information, the use of metaphor. Metaphor is a discovery tool. By forcing comparisons of unlike objects, metaphor stretches our imagination, makes us see things in a new or unusual light. It is a process that W. J. J. Gordon has called "making the familiar strange."[1] By looking at a familiar thing—a child—as though the child were a kaleidoscope, we see the child in new perspectives, say things about childhood that we wouldn't have thought of if we had merely been asked to think up a poem about the nature of childhood or think of images of childhood to be used in a poem.

By making the familiar strange, metaphor can be a powerful information-generating device. Other metaphorical figures of speech which can be useful for generating information include personal analogy, personification, oxymoron, and cross-medium comparisons using music, art, etc. Here are some examples of how these can be used to generate information for writing:

Personal Analogy: Go outside and find a tree that in some way reminds you of yourself. Now be the tree and write a description of yourself (the tree) and of what you see from where you stand. Or, as the tree, carry on an imaginary conversation with a nearby tree, a building, a passing car, etc.

Personification: Find a building that is interesting to you. Describe the build-

---

[1]   See *W. J. J. Gordon,* The Metaphorical Way of Learning and Knowing *(Cambridge, Mass.: Porpoise Books, 1971).*

ing briefly. Then consider the building to
be a living person. What would he or she
say? What would be his or her hopes and
fears, likes and dislikes? What would make
this building happy? Write as though the
building were talking.

Oxymoron: An oxymoron is a figure of
speech in which an object is given an attri-
bute which is seemingly opposite to its
nature: dry rain, gentle torture, cruel
kindness, alert sleep, cold fire, etc.
Brainstorm a list of oxymorons, choose one,
and then write a paragraph essay showing
its truth.

Cross-Medium Comparison: Think of the
following piece of music as a person. What
would he or she be like? Where and when
would the person live? What sort of clothes
would the person wear? What would be the
person's occupation? What sorts of hobbies
and pastimes might the person engage in?
Write a paragraph describing the person.
The teacher then plays a short (one minute)
exerpt from a Mozart symphony, a Brahms
quartet, Benny Goodman, etc. Music can
also be used to evoke images of places, actions, foods, animals, and so forth. Art,
especially non-representational painting
and sculpture, can be used in much the same
way.

These figures of speech work best when
the things to be compared are very much unlike each other. Crossing usual lines of
classification is a useful device. For instance, animate objects compared with in-

animate objects, active things with passive
things, natural things with artifacts. The
teacher should beware of structuring comparisons that are too pat or in which the
students may perceive the teacher looking
for one right answer. In these cases the
information-generating is likely to lapse
into a collection of cliches or cute, facile
responses. In fact, the best information-
generating sessions often occur when the
teacher has no preconceived notions about
what ideas the figure of speech will bring.

This brings us to our next information-
generating device, *random forced fit*: Draw
one slip of paper from a box containing
names of animate objects and one slip of
paper from a box containing names of inanimate objects. (These two lists could have
been previously brainstormed.) Next, brainstorm the ways that the animate object is
like the inanimate one (e.g., a sea gull is
like an old shoe). Then write a haiku, following the procedure for *The Child and the
Kaleidoscope* (see pages 12-14). Another
example of random forced fit is *The Lone
Ranger* (see page 52).

Another information generator is the
fantasy trip: "Close your eyes. Spend a
few minutes imaging that you are living in
your dream house. Where would it be? What
would it look like on the outside? Take a
tour through the house, stopping in the
livingroom, the diningroom, the kitchen,
the bedrooms. What would they be like?
What other rooms might you have? What would

the grounds around the house be like? What
special features would you include in and
around your dream house? Take a few more
minutes to look around your dream house before you open your eyes."

After two or three minutes of silence,
the teacher asks the students to open their
eyes and spend five minutes writing descriptions of their dream houses. Then the students share their paragraphs with each other
immediately, or, if the group is small enough,
the teacher reads the paragraphs and the students try to guess the author of each.

Other information-generating techniques
include the following. Possible variations
and adaptations are virtually infinite.

Observation: Spend five minutes observing the fish in the classroom's aquarium.
Take notes on what you see. Then write a
short essay on the life of a fish in a tank.

Interviews: Stand in front of the
supermarket and interview shoppers on the
price of food (or another current problem).
Keep notes. Then write an essay on your
experience, reporting on either the opinions of the shoppers interviewed or their
attitudes toward being interviewed by a
student.

Directed Reflection: Reflect on the
following questions: Where were you born?
In what place were you the happiest before
the age of twelve? Where were you the happiest during the last week? What would you
consider your home-away-from-home? If you
could go to any place in the world, but you

had to live there for a whole year, where would it be? Where would you like to be living in ten years? Then write an essay on your place in the world, using the information you have just gathered as the basis.

Unfinished Stories: The teacher reads the beginning of a story posing a problem or involving some ambiguous activity, and then asks the students to write endings to the story. This activity works best when the endings are shared immediately, either in small groups or by the whole class, and where there is an atmosphere of appreciation for each effort without an attempt to evaluate or compare.

Ambiguous Picture: The teacher shows the class a picture where the action is ambiguous and asks the class to reflect on what action took place just before the time of the picture, what action is taking place in the picture, and then what action is going to take place directly after the time of the picture. Students then write stories based on their interpretations of the picture. These stories are then shared as in *Unfinished Stories* above.

For all these activities the teacher should encourage students not to overlook potentially useful ideas because they seem to be too silly or unworkable or redundant, and to avoid the temptation to want to organize and evaluate each idea as it comes along. Some students may be anxious about "getting on with the task"—that is, writ-

ing——and the   teacher needs to encourage
these students to see collecting information as one of the most important parts of
the task of writing.

ORGANIZING INFORMATION:
     There are many excellent texts on writ-
ten composition which dwell heavily on organization. We do not attempt to duplicate
these. Rather we provide a checklist of
possible ways to arrange the great mass of
unorganized information which has been generated under Part One, above:

—Search for patterns in time/space/mater--
     ials/activities/ideas.
—Group similar items together.
—See if natural progressions exist.
—Eliminate unnecessary duplication.
—Eliminate irrelevant or unimportant items.
—Rank items in order of importance, from
     most important to least, or from least
     important to most important.
—Select the single most important item and
     arrange the other items in respect to
     it.
—Link together items which form natural
     comparisons or contrasts.
—Divide the items into general and specific
     and move deductively from general to
     specific or inductively from specific
     to general.

PRESENTING INFORMATION:

The third step of the three-step critical thinking process, presenting the information, is usually a logical and natural outcome of Step Two, *Organizing*, and in most instances the way in which the information is organized will point toward some specific end product. Depending upon the objectives of the teacher, the presentation may be designated by mode, such as narrative, descriptive, expository, or argumentative. Or it may be by genre, such as poem, play, story, essay. The medium is another important consideration. The wider variety of media considered, the more likely it is that there will be one which fits the nature of the material as well as the needs of the writer. To augment the usual written composition, it is often well worth considering other possible media for presentation: letter, newspaper, movie, videotape, speech, debate, role-play, panel discussion, extemporaneous report, impromptu lecturette, slide-tape show, bulletin board display, comic book, magazine, poster, tape recording.

Although they are sometimes overlooked, oral formats are especially useful in teaching writing. Oral reports, extemporaneous lecturettes, small and large group discussion, debating, and role-playing are all facile and effective ways for students to develop a sense of style and effectiveness. Not only do oral formats provide for immediate feedback, but they also

help students to recognize and employ a
variety and range of styles. A debater,
for instance, gains immediate feedback on
his effectiveness from the attention of
his audience, the rebuttal of his oppon-
ents, and the final outcome of the debate.
At the same time, those listening to the
debaters hear and evaluate a variety of
ways of saying things and incorporate some
of the more effective ones into their own
repertories. Thus oral formats provide for
a great deal more practice in style and
effectiveness than could be possible through
strictly written assignments. Students
benefit from oral formats by having an immediate audience with immediate feedback
and evaluation, and the teacher benefits
by being able to provide for a great deal
of practice without being overburdened with
student papers.

When the teacher feels that it is important to give students practice in actual
written expression, there are several ways
to do this without suffering the consequence
of being swamped with papers to bring home.
For instance, the teacher can divide the
students into groups of four or five and
let each student read his paper to the
others in the group. As the student reads
his paper to a live audience, problems in
communication become clear and are often
ironed out, while the self-esteem created
by having an attentive audience reinforces
the motivation to write. As variations
for the small group, the papers can be

passed around the circle: Each student reads each of the others' papers, making notes for later discussion. Another possibility is to have the students work in pairs, each person giving his or her paper to the other who then reads it back to him aloud, so that the student can hear and evaluate his own words through the filter of another person.

We suspect, however, that many teachers will want to shoulder the burden of reading their students' papers, and perhaps making comments or using correction symbols in the traditional manner. It is our opinion that this is not an effective way to teach writing nor an efficient use of the time and energy of either the teacher or the student—unless the initiative for showing the paper to the teacher comes from the student.

Where the student is motivated to improve his own writing, and when he sees the teacher as a potential helper in that process rather than as someone who is looking for reasons to give him a lower grade, then the teacher can be an effective and useful resource for the student in two significant ways: First, the teacher, by his age and experience, provides an audience which is substantially different from the student's peers; and second, the teacher is generally equipped with a capability to clarify and solve technical problems in communication.

FORCING CREATIVITY:

A forced fit of information to a particular medium is often a useful discovery tool. By having to fit the existing data into a predetermined pattern, straining against the limits of the medium, the writer often discovers new relationships and new meanings.

The *Child-Kaleidoscope Haiku* is a good example: Once the images have been brainstormed, there is a variety of possible formats for presentation—essay, free verse, short story, poster, etc. By specifying a haiku, however, the teacher frees the students from the task of determining the proper medium for the message, and allows them to focus their attention on articulating specific images within the given form.

This is an example of *forced creativity*, where constraint in one direction provides freedom in another. Creativity can be forced in this manner by limiting the number of **words** or pages or by limiting the time allowed for completion of the piece. Specifying the final form, such as a haiku or sonnet, poem in the shape of a tree, dramatic dialogue between two tombstones, etc., is another way to force creativity by constraint.

Forced creativity is the condition under which most professional writers work, whether it be a Shakespeare hammering out a play for the new season or a journeyman reporter dashing out his copy to meet a press deadline. The three-step process for critical thinking is a teaching device to promote this forced creativity. Generally, when a professional writer begins a writing task, he knows what his medium of presentation will be—often to the exact number of words; so that as he is generating and organizing his information, he is likely to be shaping his material toward its final medium. We have found, however, that for the student writer the clear separation of the writing process into its three steps makes a task which is often seen as difficult and frustrating into one which is possible and even exciting. Just imagine—students actually excited about writing about their summer vacations!

Chapter 3:

NUTS AND BOLTS

While it's all very heady to think
about making a more or less radical change
in one's teaching style, translating the
idea into action is often fraught with
doubts and numerous questions, such as
"How do I . . . ?" and *"But what do I do
if . . . ?"* With this phenomenon in mind,
we offer the following comments on imple-
menting the experience-based approach to
teaching composition.

LIMITS:
Placing limits on the dimensions or
shape or content of a piece of writing is
sometimes simply a utilitarian means of
getting a desired task accomplished within
a limited amount of class time. Frequently,
however, these limits are designed to re-
lease creativity and reduce the student's
risk of failure.
A concern for perfection is often an
immobilizing force against student writers.
Fearing that their very best efforts may
not be good enough, students often are re-

luctant to start a writing assignment or engage half-heartedly, with lowered energy. Two devices that are used in this book to reduce the immobilizing properties of this concern for perfection are the use of time limits and imposed structure.

Limiting the time allows the student to concentrate on the task, just doing as much as the allotted time permits, no need to worry about getting it perfect. In this sense, the time limit is an alibi for being human.

Imposing structure, such as a certain form of verse or a maximum number of words for an essay, also reduces the concern for perfection. The teacher in effect accepts some of the responsibility for the assignment, thus freeing the student from having to be perfect.

Some such limitations are used as aids to creativity—as means of releasing the student writer from an excessive burden of decision-making in order to concentrate on one particular aspect of a large problem. If the form for a short poem is dictated, for example, then the student is freed from trying to decide what form would be most appropriate for his subject and can concentrate his efforts on the next step of the writing process. If his subject is limited to *one* tree in the woods, he is then free to explore that tree in much greater depth and detail than if he felt responsible for the entire forest. In a very real sense the student writer is freer to create within the restrictions placed on him than he would be without them.

PUBLIC WRITING—PRIVATE WRITING:
Most of the activities in this book are designed as public writing—pieces that can probably be shared without the risk of embarrassment or the threat of over-sensitive self-revelation. The teacher should be explicit, however, as to whether the assignment is to be public writing or private—for the student's eyes alone. When a student is asked to jot down the twenty things he loves most to do, he may be wary of listing some of his most personal items unless he is assured that the list is private writing, that he will not be forced to show his paper to anyone else or to hand it in to the teacher at the end of the period.

PUBLISHING:
Seeing one's own words in print or hearing them on tape is always exciting. Teachers can help to stimulate their students toward writing by publishing the work of each of their students whenever possible. Class newspapers and magazines, a loose-leaf class anthology, letters to the editor, stories for children's magazines, and the bulletin board are all possible ways of getting student writing into print.
Tape-recording is another useful publishing device. Students are fascinated

by hearing their own writings and the writings of their classmates recorded on tape by the teacher or another reader. The mechanical device of playing back from a tape recorder seems to be more effective than simply reading the papers directly to the class. While the tape is being played, the teacher does not have to be the performer, but is instead an appreciative member of the audience.

Teachers should avoid, however, the temptation to use such published writings as examples of errors in style or mechanics. The instructional benefits of such uses are almost always outweighed by the damage to future motivation.

LETTER WRITING:

Letter writing is one means of achieving an authentic outside audience. We know a teacher who designates each Thursday as "Letter Writing Day." When the students come into class on that day, they can sit down and start writing any letter they choose, knowing that they will have the entire period to write letters. The teacher serves as a resource for helping with spelling and punctuation, when students want help, and as an address bank to help students find the addresses of sports and movie stars, public officials, etc. The teacher also uses the period to catch up on his own letter writing, serving as a model for what he expects of the students.

The list of possibilities for letter

writing is almost infinite: friends and
former friends, relatives, friends of parents, shop keepers, local public officials,
state and national governmental officials,
newspaper and magazine editors (with the
chance that the letter will be published),
authors, movie and television stars, and
sports figures. Letters to these audiences
are usually answered, often personally.

Also there are pen-pal arrangements
with foreign or distant students and letters
to persons who are confined in hospitals,
convalescent homes, or prisons, or to persons serving in the armed forces.

Letter writing is a useful means to
start the creative flow of writing and to
give opportunities for practicing writing
for an authentic audience. We have found
that letter writing best serves these pur-
poses when the teacher accepts the work of
the students in good faith and therefore
refrains from checking outgoing letters
for mechanics, style, or effort.

INTERDEPENDENCE AND COLLABORATION:
Many of the writing activities included
in this book involve students working in
groups and achieving a group project. This
approach troubles some teachers who are
used to the norms of independent work and
put a premium on individual effort and accomplishment. Others are troubled that
some students may not pull their weight in
a group situation and therefore may "get
away with something."

We take the position that the ability to work fruitfully with others towards a common purpose is a crucial skill for our civilization—a survival skill. Much of human activity today, especially in vocational situations, requires active collaboration. As to technical skills in writing, group work gives the opportunity for much more verbalization, both written and oral—with immediate feedback and opportunities for reworking and retrial, than does the standard class format.

While some of each student's writing should represent independent work, of course, much of the work of learning to write can be done productively through active collaboration.

"THIS IS SILLY":

Occasionally a traditionally oriented student may balk at doing an activity because "This is silly," or "What does this have to do with learning how to write?" We feel that it is most important to hear students out and to deal with their concerns in this regard. None of the activities has absolute virtue in itself, and no student should be forced to do an activity that he feels is silly, inconsequential, beneath his dignity, or not to the point.

In dealing with this situation the teacher can re-examine his objectives for using the activity, share these with the student, and then together with the student plan an alternate assignment to carry out those objectives.

CORRECTIONS:

Don't do it! It is our opinion that most students learn style, usage, and mechanics in spite of, rather than because of, all those red marks that teachers put on their papers. Furthermore, there is no motivation for improving except the fear of bad grades and teacher disapproval, and fear is generally an ineffective motivating force in the long run.

See Chapter Nine, "Mechanics."

GRADING:

Don't do it. Despite myths to the contrary, people in the "real world" aren't graded on their writing. Professional writing is never graded. It may be accepted or rejected for publication on the basis of its merit, but in this case the motivation for writing acceptable material comes from the author. Professional writing may be criticized, but we've never yet seen a professional critic give a book a *B+* for content and a *C* for style. Furthermore, the critic is speaking not to the author but to his prospective readership.

See Chapter Eleven, "Evaluation."

REVISION:

Many English teachers hold revision to be an absolute virtue, along with God, Mother, and the topic sentence. At the

risk of losing half our readership, we suggest that much of what students write should
not be revised.   This is not to suggest
that revision is not important—it is ex-
tremely important at appropriate times.
And those times are when the piece is to
be prepared for public display and scrutiny,
when the author has a vested interest in
having his words understood and his meaning known.   When these conditions do not
exist, then insistence on revision is requiring sacrifice before an impotent idol.
It breeds contempt for the practice and
for the person who forces the sacrifice.
The motivation for revision should come
from the writer, just as should the motivation for writing.   The teacher can help
the student to want to revise by pointing
out the reasons for revising under particular circumstances.

USING THIS BOOK:
     The *Compendium of Activities* which
follows is divided into four sections: A
number of activities involving the partic-
ipation of the whole class in an experience
which generates raw material to be followed
by individual and/or small group writing.
Some activities requiring scissors, glue,
and construction paper and old magazines
which can produce either written or oral
composition (or both).   A collection of
short poetry forms which can be used in
conjunction with a wide variety of pre-
liminary exercises.   And some longer-term

projects, for both individuals and groups,
which call for a sustained commitment of
time and energy.

In the first section of the *Compendium*
the presentation of each activity includes
necessary materials, procedures, technical
objectives, and possible extensions and
variations. The listings of technical objectives are not necessarily either defin-
itive or complete; they are included with
the hope that they will be helpful, especially to teachers who must plan in terms
of performance objectives.

There is nothing final or in any way
sacred about the activities included in
this book. It is our hope that teachers
will feel free to adapt this material to
their own needs and teaching styles. What
we offer here is something to start with,
a foundation on which teachers—and students—can build their own unique composition programs.

II:

A COMPENDIUM OF ACTIVITIES

Chapter 4:

ACTIVITIES FOR THE WHOLE CLASS

THE OCCLUDOSCOPE:
   Materials: One or more occludoscopes.
(This is a simple homemade device consisting of a paper towel roll or mailing tube
and a cardboard box. Cut holes in opposite
sides of the box so that the tube can be
fitted through. The tube should be in the
approximate center of the box and parallel
to the base of the box.)
   Procedure: Place the occludoscope on
a table and ask a volunteer to come forward
and describe what he sees through the tube,
*making no assumptions about what he cannot
see.* Students will find this quite hard
at first. For instance, if the student says
that he sees the back of a chair, he is
making an assumption that the rest of the
chair (which he cannot see) exists.
   From this point, the occludoscope has

many possible uses, depending upon the number available, the make-up of the class, and the objectives of the teacher:

Forfeit: One person goes to the occludoscope and describes as much as he can. He may keep looking through the occludoscope and describing until someone catches him making an assumption, at which point he is sent down, and the person who caught him may take his place. NOTE: The person looking through the occludoscope may move the focus from time to time, but he may look through it only when it is in position and stationary.

Dictation: The class is divided into groups of three, each with an occludoscope. The first student dictates a short paragraph describing what he sees to the second student, while the third judges for assumptions. After the first student has finished his dictation, the students change places and repeat the process until all have had a turn as describer, recorder, and judge. NOTE: The occludoscope may be moved between turns so that a new view is opened for each student.

Guess: This is an open classroom type of activity which works best when not everybody wants to use the occludoscopes at the same moment. Three occludoscopes are taped in stationary positions. Then students divide into pairs. Each student writes a brief description of what he sees through each occludoscope on a separate card. He then hands his three cards to his partner,

who tries to guess which description goes
with which occludoscope.

Technical Objectives: Awareness of
detail and relationships, description, use
of concrete images.

Variations and Extensions: Take the
occludoscope outdoors: Describe the grass
(it may not be green) or the bark of a tree,
or a part of a cloud. Try an occludoscope
walk (a variation of a blind walk, where
you are limited to what you can see out of
the occludoscope).

CARD TOWER:
Materials: Used computer cards, masking tape.

Procedure: The class is divided into
groups of four. Each group receives a stack
of one hundred used computer cards and a
roll of masking tape. Then the teacher
gives the following instructions:

"You are to build a tower made from
the computer cards and tape to be judged
on the basis of height, stability, and
originality of design. You will have fifteen minutes to plan and build your structure. You may spend as much of your time
as you want in planning, or you may begin
to build immediately, but your total time
will be limited to fifteen minutes. I will
advise you of the time every five minutes
and also one minute before the fifteen minutes are over. Ready? Go."

At the end of the fifteen minutes, the
teacher calls time and allows the students

to move from structure to structure, observing each of the other structures. Then on separate pieces of paper, each student writes one sentence telling what he likes best about each structure, including his own. All the sentences about each tower are collected and given to the group that built that tower to read.

Technical Objectives: Positive criticism, use of detail, comparison and contrast.

Variations and Extensions: Each student can be asked to write a paragraph or two describing how the group worked together to plan and build the tower. These paragraphs can be read in the small groups.

Suppose a new group of students, one which has never seen the tower, is about to duplicate the construction. Without resorting to pictures or diagrams, write a set of instructions to them so that they can duplicate this tower. (This can be either an individual or a group writing project.) If possible, the instructions should then be tested in action by having another group actually try to duplicate the tower from the written instructions.

SHOES:

Materials: One shoe per participant.

Procedure: The class sits in a circle, and each member throws his right shoe into the middle of the circle. Then the teacher asks for one or two volunteers to organize the shoes into one line, according to some principle of classification. The volunteers might take an historical perspective, for instance, putting the more basic, fundamental types first, or a service perspective, placing the most utilitarian at one end, the most ornamental at the other, or use some principle such as size or color. While the volunteers are organizing the shoes, the other members of the class should be giving advice, making comments on other possible relationships, or generally kibitzing on the process. (If the class is large, it may be divided into two smaller groups to simplify the task of the volunteers.)

When the shoes have been arranged, then the students are asked to reflect upon their own shoes—the shoe's position in relation to the total line, its neighbors, and where it might like to be if it had its free choice. Then the teacher asks each student to become his shoe and write a brief paragraph describing himself, the shoe.

Technical Objectives: Organization, use of analogy, descriptive writing, use of specific detail.

Variations and Extensions: Focus on the two shoes at the extreme ends of the line: Compare them. Give examples of specific situations where one or the other would be more appropriate.

Brainstorm additional ways to classify and arrange the shoes.

What is the relationship between girls' shoes and boys' shoes? Can they be arranged together, or should they be separate?

Write a dialogue between two represen-
tative shoes discussing why their owners
chose them.

FIRST PERSON NEWS STORY:

Materials: Several newspapers.

Procedure: The class is divided into
groups of four or five, and the teacher
assigns to each group a story from a newspaper. One member of each group reads the
story aloud, and then, working individually,
each student rewrites the story as though
he were one of the principals involved or
an eye witness. The members of the group
then share their stories with one another.

This activity works best when the
teacher prepares the class by reading one
news story and then discussing the tone
and point-of-view and making suggestions
as to how it could be rewritten as a personal narrative.

The activity can also be done with the
entire class using the same story or with
each class member choosing a different story.

Technical Objectives: Narrative writing, point-of-view, tone, objectivity and
subjectivity.

Variations and Extensions: Brainstorm
images that come to mind during the reading
of the news story, and then compose a haiku,
lune, or other short poem based on the incident.

The activity can be reversed by giving
a fictional story or a poem and asking the
students to recast the piece as a news story.

METAMORPHOSIS:

> *Materials:* None.

> *Procedure:* Suppose you suddenly turned
into one of the objects in this room—the
chair you're sitting in, the desk, the blackboard, a poster on the wall. What would
you be thinking about? What would be your
hopes and dreams? What could others do for
you to make you happy? What would you fear?
What would you like to do best? Choose an
object in this room, study it, and then
write a paragraph or two introducing yourself to the class as that object.

> *Technical Objectives:* Organization,
use of detail, use of first person point-
of-view.

> *Variations and Extensions:* Pick an
object from your livingroom, from a picture,
from outside. Change into an animal, a car,
etc. Become an abstraction such as truth,
beauty, goodness, hate, evil, justice.
Change into a city or a country.

ARRANGED INCIDENT:

> *Materials:* A pre-arranged, WRITTEN
script and whatever costumes and/or properties it calls for.

> Since the incident is to interrupt the
"normal" program of the class, it must be
an attention-grabber, either through the
appearance of the principal actor or by his
or her actions (or possibly both). For an
ordinary single class period, it is probably
best to use only one actor, who can be a
maintenance man, a volunteer parent, another

teacher, or a student. It is of utmost importance that the script be followed with
absolute accuracy. To that end, a rehearsal
or two beforehand would be desirable.

   Procedure: The class begins in the
customary manner. At a pre-arranged time
or on a clandestine signal the script is
carried out in the classroom. As soon as
it is over, the teacher (or someone else
if the teacher has been very much involved
in the preceding incident) instructs the
class: "What happened? Don't tell me,
don't talk about it, write it down: What
happened? Don't confer with anyone else
at this stage. Just write down as com-
pletely and accurately as you can what has
just happened. Include as many details as
you can. Your purpose is to get the facts
in writing, not to write a polished composition." (The important thing here is
to get them to explode onto paper instead
of to each other.)

   When nearly everyone seems to be almost finished (or earlier if you are very
pinched for time), announce that there will
be one more minute in which to finish up or
make additional notes. Then, when time is
called, ask students to form pairs and compare notes on what happened. Each pair
should make a list of points on which they
cannot agree. If there is adequate time,
at this point pairs can combine into fours
and repeat the process.

   When discussion seems to have gone as
far as it profitably can, each pair or

group should list on the blackboard the
points upon which agreement was *not* reached.
The next step is the check against reality.
This can be done by restaging the incident,
by handing out dittoed copies of the script,
or both, or by having the principal actor
return for questioning. It is most important that adequate time be allowed for discussion of differences in perceptions caused
by the physical locations of the observers
and other variable factors and of at least
some of the hidden assumptions behind "objective" reporting.

Technical Objectives: Awareness of
environment, of details. Recognizing assumptions behind "objective" statements.
Variations in point of view. Accuracy of
description and reporting without assumptions. Coping with the problem of simul-
taneous actions in narration.

Variations and Extensions: After the
writing have a "detective" appear and ask
questions about what happened and about the
appearance of the principal participant in
the incident. A show of hands as to points
of controversy such as color of eyes or
hair, whether or not wearing a necktie,
etc., indicates differing viewpoints and
assumptions.

Hand out a dittoed sheet of detective's
questions with multiple choice or true-
false answers. After a short work period
the answers can be easily tabulated and
displayed on the blackboard, then to be
verified by the reality test, as above.

If a double period or some other extended period of time can be arranged, a more elaborate script can be prepared, using two or three characters. Procedures would be the same as those for the simpler incident with allowance for more time for writing and discussion at each stage in proportion to the complexity of the incident staged.

UTOPIA:

Materials: None.

Procedure: What would the world be like if it were perfect? Students brainstorm for five minutes what would be the features of a perfect world, the ideas being recorded on the blackboard. Then the students, working individually, are asked to pick one aspect of life, such as food, shelter, clothes, transportation, friendships, school, or work, and write a paragraph of no more than fifty words describing that aspect of utopia. The paragraphs can be shared immediately or be collected into a travelogue book of utopia.

Technical Objectives: Unity, emphasis, expository writing, use of detail.

Variations and Extensions: The brainstormed material can be worked into a poem, either with constraints, such as a haiku, or as free verse.

The class can produce a much more extensive work concerning the utopia and those living there—stories, plays, criticisms about the quality of life in Utopia, etc.

FABLES:

    Materials: None.

    Procedure: Why should we be honest? Not steal? Be generous or kind? The teacher reads the class one or two of Aesop's *Fables.* Then the class brainstorms virtues and vices, the list being recorded on the board. Each student then takes a virtue or vice from the list and writes a little fable which shows the importance of living by the virtue or refraining from the vice. The fables are then shared with the class.

    Technical Objectives: Narrative writing. Cause and effect. Descriptive writing.

    Variations and Extensions: The class can put together a book of fables. The original list can be used to formulate a new "Ten Commandments." The fables can be worked into plays, possibly with a narrator to point out the moral lesson.

MODERN MYTHS:

    Materials: None.

    Procedure: What are the stars? What makes the rivers run? Where does the snow come from? Why does it get dark at night? The teacher asks the class to imagine that no scientific explanations exist to answer these questions. If the class is unfamiliar with mythology, the teacher may also read them a myth explaining some natural phenomenon, such as the Persephone myth.

    The class brainstorms natural phenomena. Then, after selecting one phenomenon to work on, the class divides into groups

of four or five to brainstorm mythical explanations for the phenomenon. Each group
writes up its explanation, which is then
shared with the class.

 Technical Objectives: Narrative writing. Cause and effect writing.

 Variations and Extensions: Each group
can select a different natural phenomenon,
and the class can produce a book of myths.

 The myths can be made into short plays
which can be performed for the whole class
or for an audience of younger children.

 Individuals can each select a different
natural phenomenon to explain. To give
unity to the project, the class might work
up a set of mythic characters—gods and
heroes—and then all of the myths would
have to use these characters in explaining the phenomena.

CLASS HOLIDAY:
 Materials: None.
 Procedure: If the class could declare
its own holiday, what would it want to celebrate? Balloon Day? Chocolate Ice Cream
Sunday? Ball Point Pen Day? The class
brainstorms for five minutes on new holiday possibilities. Then, by vote, one is
chosen. In groups of four or five, the
students then brainstorm happenings and
customs to be connected with the holiday.
Then each group writes its description of
how the holiday is to be celebrated.

 Technical Objectives: Expository
writing. Narrative writing. Specific detail.

Variations and Extensions: After the initial brainstorm, each group can choose a different holiday to elaborate. Then the work of the class can be compiled into a book of holidays.

Letters can be written to the newspaper suggesting the establishment of such a holiday.

The holiday suggestions can be restricted to commercial possibilities, such as General Motors Day or Prince Spaghetti Day, and then the descriptions can be sent to the president of the company involved.

CUSTOMS OF THE NATIVES:
Materials: None.
Procedure: When an outsider visits a foreign culture, he often discovers that the everyday habits of the people are different from those of his own culture. Many travelers have written of the "curious customs of the natives," describing these foreign habits and often trying to give an explanation for them.

Suppose that a stranger arrived at your school. What would he observe as the "curious customs of the natives"? The gatherings around the lockers in the mornings? The bells that suddenly call everyone into the halls? The curious seating arrangements in the rooms? If he had no real knowledge as to what was going on in the school, what explanations might he make up for these curious customs?

To introduce the subject, the teacher

may wish to read a passage from *The Adventures of Marco Polo*, Melville's *Typee*, *Gulliver's Travels*, etc.

Next the class brainstorms what an outsider might consider to be the curious customs of their school.

Then each student writes a short travel piece from the point of view of an outsider, describing some of these curious customs and trying to explain them. The pieces are then shared in class.

Technical Objectives: Narrative and expository writing. Cause and effect. Use of detail. Comparison and contrast.

Variations and Extensions: Each student or group of three or four can take a different curious custom to elaborate upon and explain, and then all the pieces can be collected into a book describing the school.

Students can brainstorm and write up the "curious customs" of their families; curious customs of the television world or of television commercials; curious customs of the strange event called football; curious customs associated with the strange machine called automobile; and so forth.

TOPICAL QUESTIONS:

Materials: It's hard to predict what will be the topic of concern on the American scene at any particular time, but it is certain that there will almost always be at least one item of interest to use for a topical question. Recently for instance, the interest in ecology has produced questions such as how can we recycle more effectively? How can we reduce air, noise, water pollution? How can we save open spaces while providing for a growing population? The energy crisis has produced questions such as how can we save on oil heat? How can we cut our electrical consumption? How can we use our automobiles less? Topical questions such as these provide interesting material for brainstorming, discussion, and writing.

Procedure: The class brainstorms possible solutions to a topical question, being sure to include as many far-fetched, zany ideas as possible. Then the students are given a choice of three writing assignments: (1) A letter to the local newspaper suggesting practical ways that the community can deal with the problem. (2) An editorial to submit to the school newspaper with suggestions for action by the school community. Or (3) a fictional piece about a person who tries all the zany, far-fetched ideas to deal with the problem.

Technical Objectives: Argumentative writing. Narrative. Letter writing. Editorial writing.

Variations and Extensions: The brainstorming can be done in groups of four or five, with each group making a report to the entire class at the end of a ten minute period. Or each group can write a satirical account of a person who tries all of the far-fetched ideas developed by that group,

the accounts to be read to the entire class
at the end of the period.

Targets of special influence can be
identified, such as the beer industry, the
soft drink industry (in the case of ecology),
or the outdoor advertising association (in
the case of the energy crisis), and students
can write letters to leaders of these groups
urging specific action to remedy the situation.

Students might mount a local campaign
with leaflets, posters, and rallies with
speeches urging local citizens to buy only
returnable bottles, to bring reusable shop-
ping bags to market, or to take specific
energy conservation measures, for example.

Another area of topical questions
would include such questions as how to
put the "thanks" back into Thanksgiving.
How best to observe Veterans' Day? Etc.

BIRTHDAYS:
Materials: A reference library with
periodicals and newspapers.

Procedure: What was the world like
on the day that you were born? What were
the big news items? What did automobiles
look like? What did people wear? What was
the weather? What was the important television or radio program or sporting event
of the day?

This is a project that should be done
over a period of several days so that the
local library is not swamped. The teacher
explains how and where to find back news-

papers and periodicals in the library and then asks the students to do research on the day that they were born for a report.

To prepare for the assignment, the class might brainstorm interesting questions and then discuss possible ways of finding the answers. To complete their research students might interview their fathers or mothers for first-hand accounts of the important day. Then the reports can be prepared—as a newspaper story, an essay, or a sort of travelogue in time. The final reports should be shared in class, and they may also be bound into a book.

Technical Objectives: The use of the library. Research. Preparing for research—asking the right questions, determining sources of information. Expository writing.

Variations and Extensions: What was the world like on one of your parents' birthday? Pick a parent and do the same kind of research on his or her birthday. Then do a report comparing the world then with the world when you were born.

What was the world like when your parent (or teacher) was the age you are now? Add your present age to your parent's birth date and look up what the world was like then. You may wish to interview your parent as well: What subjects was he or she taking in school? Which did he or she find the hardest? What sorts of extra-curricular activities did he or she take part in? How did he or she spend his or

her free time? Weekends? Summer vacation?
Then write a report comparing your world
and life today with that of your parent at
the same age.

NOTE: It should be emphasized that
the term *report* is used here without reference to form, mode, genre, or medium of
presentation.

THE LONE RANGER:

Materials: None.

NOTE: It is said that Frank Striker,
the creator of *The Lone Ranger* on radio, had
five boxes on his desk filled with ideas
for "Heroes," "Villains," "Obstacles," "Ways
to Overcome Obstacles," and "Settings."
Each week he would reach into each box and
draw out a slip of paper and then construct
the next episode from this random selection.

Procedure: The class brainstorms lists
of Heroes, Villains, Obstacles, Ways to
Overcome Obstacles, and Settings. Then by
random selection each student takes one item
from each list and writes a short narrative,
fitting the pieces into a story. The stories
are then shared in small groups or with the
whole class.

For random selection, slips can be prepared and drawn from boxes. Or each list
can be numbered 0-9, and then each student
takes the items corresponding to the last
five digits in his telephone number.

Technical Objectives: Narrative writing. Cause and effect explanation.

Variations and Extensions: As an open classroom activity, the slips of paper can be prepared and placed in labeled boxes. Then students choose a slip from each box and do the writing at their own pace.

As a group activity, each group of four or five can draw one slip from each category and then compose the story as a group effort. Each group should then read its story to the entire class.

Chapter 5:

SCISSORS AND GLUE ACTIVITIES[1]

The activities in this chapter use the old magazines, newspapers, and books of our civilization—as a rich source of raw material to be articulated into new meaningful patterns, mostly without pencil or pen, but rather with scissors, glue, and construction paper.

Collages, clipped poems, and the like may be called fun and games by some, but let's look at some of the technical writing skills that this kind of activity promotes: First is organization—the ability to collect relevant information, to sort it out, and to place it in some meaningful order. Second, the use of metaphor and the connotative meaning of words and pictures. Metaphor is a discovery tool, and by straining against

_____

[1] *This chapter is adapted from "Scissors, Glue, and English, Too," published in* The Independent School Bulletin, *October 1973. Copyright 1973 by the National Association of Independent Schools. Used with permission.*

the limitations of the medium, in this case
working with fixed words and pictures, the
creation forces the creator to be newly
aware of relationships and symbolic meanings. Third, the use of imagery to illustrate a point. The words and the pictures
used in these activities show the power of
concrete imagery. Other technical areas
such as emphasis, balance, harmony, juxtaposition, phrasing, and even grammar come
into play as students manipulate words and
pictures into meaningful patterns, and then
discuss their intentions and rationales
with the product on display.

In addition to technical writing skills,
these activities promote personal learning
in several important ways. First, because
the medium is so facile, the activities
foster positive self-concepts, especially
in lower ability students, who at once see
the opportunity to succeed. Also, the mani-
pulation of materials is in itself clarifying
to the self-concepts. Students make discoveries about themselves through force-
fitting the pictures and words into a meaningful pattern. Students develop their
ability to empathize through studying pictures and linking the facial expressions
and body language that they observe with
verbal expression. And finally, through
the sharing of these creations with each
other in small groups or in the class, students learn more about their uniquenesses
and commonalities, about how they are per-
ceived by others, and about how they affect

other people. In fact, these activities
bear in heavily on questions such as Who
am I? What are my values? What place do
I have in this world?

When using scissors and glue activities
for the first time, it is well for the teacher to be quite explicit to the class about
the value of the activity, particularly in
terms of technical skills. Students, especially by the time they arrive at junior
high school, are often set in their expectations of what an English class should be.
Fast section, achievement-oriented, college-
bound students may see these activities as
a waste of their time, something that will
not contribute to their scores on the College
Board exams. Slow sections, on the other
hand, may see these activities as conde-
scending—after all, scissors and glue is
elementary school stuff, and they feel that
they should be beyond that now. The problem of handling student expectations is,
of course, an individual one: No two classes
are exactly alike. One possible course is
for the teacher to ask the class to brainstorm the possible technical skills that
such assignments could foster, and then
the teacher might fill in the list with
suggestions of his own.

SELF COLLAGES—REAL SELF, IDEAL SELF:
   Materials: Old magazines, construction paper, scissors, glue.
   Procedure: This is a double assignment, producing two collages—one repre-

senting the person's real self, the other representing the person's ideal self. Because each collage takes between thirty minutes and an hour to construct, these are often best given as homework assignments or as open classroom activities.

The assignment is for each student to pick at random one magazine and from it make a collage in words and pictures which represents his real self. Then, working from the same magazine or selecting one new magazine, the student makes a second collage which represents his ideal self. When the collages are finished, they can be shared in small groups or posted on the wall.

As an intriguing extension, the teacher can collect the collages after they have been displayed for a week or so and store them until the end of the term. At the end of the term the teacher passes out the collages and asks each student to reflect on how he/she has changed or grown during the term. (We know one teacher who has used this as part of her final exam.)

Notes: Having the students select one magazine at random keeps them from getting bogged down in searching through all the magazines for just the right picture or phrase. Since the student has to work with a limited supply of material he must make a force-fit between his preconceived notions and the material at hand, and this is where discoveries are made.

Limiting the time is another useful

device. By limiting the time to forty minutes and giving a warning ten minutes before the finishing time, the teacher can
reduce the personal risk to the student—
after all, no one is expected to produce
a perfect work when faced with such a short
time limit.

CLIPPED POEMS:
     Each student selects one old magazine
and then cuts out words, phrases, and sentences that interest him in some way. The
student then glues the clippings on a piece
of paper in an arrangement that can be read
as a poem. If a refrain is needed, one of
the phrases can be written in at appropriate
intervals. The poem doesn't have to rhyme,
of course, but there should be some kind of
unity.
     The poems are shared in small groups
or with the class as a whole. They may
then be posted on the bulletin board or
made into a magazine.
     To make the assignment more challeng-
ing, some students may wish to select words
and phrases from only ten or twelve consec-
utive pages.
     As a variation for sharing, one person
in each group can read all of the poems for
that group anonymously, while the group
members try to guess who wrote which poem.

THEME COLLAGE:
     A collage can be done on any theme
such as freedom, war, love, peace. An ex-

tension of the *Theme Collage* is to have half
the class make "war" collages and the other
half make "peace" collages and then to post
the two themes on different sections of the
wall. The students are then asked to examine one theme at a time and see what seem
to be the common attributes of that theme
as expressed by the collected collages.
Then the class can discuss the two lists
of attributes for the opposing themes,
noting similarities and differences.

EMPHASIS COLLAGE:

This activity serves to make students
more aware of unity and emphasis in composition. Each student selects a theme such
as love, poverty, or freedom. Then each
decides privately what point he wishes to
emphasize in regard to his theme. (For
example, love is often superficial in our
society, freedom requires responsibility,
etc.) The students then build their collages
to emphasize those points.

When the collages are all completed
and labeled as to main theme (this is often
best done at home), students form groups of
three or four, and each student passes his
collage to another person in the group.
Then each student spends three or four minutes examining the collage in front of him
and jotting down notes about what the collage
is pointing out. The process is repeated
until each group member has "read" each
other member's collage. Then the collages
are passed back to their creators, along

with the notes from the "readers." Small
group discussion can follow.

This activity creates a responsive and
immediate audience for short pieces of writing (the notes) as well as giving immediate
feedback to each person as to the effect of
his message on others.

SELF IN FIVE YEARS COLLAGE:

Students are asked to make collages
that represent what they hope they will be
like in five years. Then in discussing the
collages, students might be asked what they
can start doing now so that their hopes may
be realized in five years.

LITERATURE COLLAGE:

This is an extension of the theme
collage. Students are asked to make a
collage representing a theme or character
from a work of literature that they have
studied. Then the others in the class might
be asked to guess what aspect or which character from the work the collage represents.

The teacher may need to give a little
instruction on the modernizing of period
characters. For instance, it would be
difficult to do a collage representing
Sidney Carton in *A Tale of Two Cities* trying to get only pictures of late eighteenth
century London and Paris settings. Instead,
the collage might represent the essential
qualities of Sidney Carton as they might
be symbolized in the modern world. This
kind of modernizing has the additional bene-

fit of linking the work of literature with today, pointing up its relevance.

FACES AND CAPTIONS:

Students work in groups of four. Each student starts a cartoon sequence by cutting out a face or figure and pasting it on the left-hand side of a piece of construction paper. Then each passes his paper along to the right so that each student has a new piece of paper with a picture of a face or figure on the left side.

Each person looks at the picture in front of him, makes up something that that character should be saying, writes it in as a cartoon bubble coming from that face's mouth, and then passes the paper along. The third step adds a new face on the right-hand side of the paper to respond to the picture and caption on the left. The papers are passed again, and the fourth and final step is to make up a response to the first caption, which will be the quotation for the second picture. The result is four different two-picture cartoons with a caption or cartoon bubble for each picture.

This can also be done by one person alone or by two persons, with each person doing two of the steps, or with three persons, with the third person doing steps three and four.

The results are generally amusing, often quite hilarious. Students have the opportunity to collaborate on a piece of writing while learning about juxtaposition, contrast,

thesis and antithesis, empathy, and so on.
This activity takes a relatively short period
of time and can be done in the last half of
a period where the focus was on something
else.

ADVERTOONS:
        This activity is similar to *Faces and
Captions*, except that the quotations are all
clippings found in magazines—no original
writing is allowed. Generally one person
does the whole advertoon, often starting
with a question or a command cut from an
advertisement. The phrase should be cut in
the form of a balloon which can be pasted
onto the picture of a person to indicate
that that is what the person is saying. The
rest of the faces and captions are responses
to the initial question or command. Advertoons often turn into small books, with the
question or command on the first page and
then a page for each of the responses.

THE FUTURE IS . . . :
        The class brainstorms for five minutes
on completions to a metaphor such as "The
future is . . ." or "Fear is . . ." or
"Love is . . . ." During the brainstorming period the class should strive for as
many ideas as possible, with the teacher
encouraging zany, far-out ideas and writing each idea, no matter what it is, on the
blackboard. When the five minutes are up
(if the blackboard won't hold all the ideas,
use newsprint and magic markers to supple-

ment—don't erase early ideas), each student selects privately eight or ten ideas that are especially interesting or amusing to him and writes them down on a piece of paper.

Next each student looks through old magazines for pictures, one to illustrate each of his metaphors, gluing the pictures to construction paper and writing the metaphor under each picture. The pages can be stapled together to make books entitled *The Future Is . . .*, etc. Then students share their books with one another. One of the fascinations of sharing the books is in finding out how others handled the same material.

STORY COLLAGE:

This is a group story-telling project. Two boxes are prepared, one containing interesting pictures, the other interesting phrases, clipped from magazines. The boxes are placed at the front of the room and a large piece of paper is taped on the wall. One student goes forward, draws a clipping from one of the two boxes, pastes it on the wall, and starts to tell a story using the clipping as his subject. The next student comes forward, draws a picture or phrase, pastes it on the wall, and continues the story, using the new clipping in his portion. The process is repeated until the story reaches a natural conclusion. At the end of the story, a new story may be started so that all students may have a chance to participate in the process.

FOUND PLAYS:

Each student clips from a magazine or newspaper four phrases which are interesting to him in some way. Then the students form groups of three, and the teacher gives the following instructions:

"Each group now has twelve phrases to work with. Your task is to combine those phrases in any manner you wish in order to make a short play involving three characters, which you will perform. You may make up a title for your play if you wish, and you may make up two lines of original dialogue if you wish. After you have made up the play, you should spend the rest of the time rehearsing so that you will be able to present your play to the class. You have the next half hour for preparing your play."

This activity helps to point out the use of expressive gestures and actions in story-telling. Generally, the activity works best when there is a double period so that the plays can be performed on the same day that they are conceived.

PICTURE THEATER:

This activity can be used to highlight the several levels of significance in a play or movie. The teacher may wish to start with a short discussion of the various levels of significance in a play such as the level of facts—plot, events; the

level of social situation—class, historic
setting; the aesthetic level—scenery, music;
the psychological level—inner action, feel-
ings, motivations; etc. Citing specific
popular movies or TV shows as illustrations
is helpful. Then the class is divided into
groups of three.

Each group selects a picture from a
magazine which implies a dramatic situation
of some kind. Then they exchange pictures
with another group so that each group has a
new picture to work with. Then the groups
try to decide what took place immediately
before the time of the picture or what will
take place immediately after it, and each
group develops a short dramatic scene, including as many of the levels previously
discussed as possible in their planning.

The written form of the scene can vary
from a bare minimum of notes to a fully
developed scenario or even, if occasion
and materials warrant, a full-scale dramatic scene with written dialogue and stage
directions. Every member of the group must
be involved in the scene (even if only one
person was shown in the picture). Then the
students rehearse their scenes and present
them to the class.

FANTASY WALL:
A *Fantasy Wall* is similar to a graffitti
wall, except that material such as old magazines, scissors, paste, crayons, and other
art materials are available. One section
of wall is covered with butcher paper, news-

print, or something similar, and the materials are provided in boxes or on a table near the wall. This can be an on-going or open classroom activity where students who have finished other projects may come to spend varying amounts of time working on the huge collage.

From time to time the class may wish to discuss aesthetic problems connected with the wall such as balance, harmony, emphasis, and the question of when it should be declared finished. Once the collage has been declared finished, then it might be left up for a week or two while a new collage is started on another wall, or it may be taken down and saved for a mammoth display towards the end of the year.

Fantasy Walls can be done on single themes such as freedom or hopes for the future; or impressions from literature can be used. Another possibility is to have two fantasy walls side by side or on opposite walls, each representing a contrasting theme such as war and peace, or liberal and conservative, or comedy and tragedy.

This activity generally works best when there are other activities going on at the same time so that not everybody is trying to work on the wall at once.

While some teachers may wish to use some of these activities as stimuli for formal composition assignments, we have found that it is usually best to let the lessons of organization, critical thinking, self-concepts clarification, and the like emerge indirectly from the interest and discussion generated by the activities themselves. Unless the class is highly motivated towards writing (as in a creative writing elective, for instance), the attempt to tie each activity to a formal written composition may prove counterproductive for two reasons: First, the students come to mistrust such activities, since they realize that they will be forced to write about them afterwards, and second, they regard the activities not as valuable in their own right, but merely as gimmicks to use as composition topics. This devaluation of their own personal experience by means of an externally imposed requirement is one of the causes of the apathy and low self-esteem apparent in many students today. The value of these scissors-and-glue activities is that they promote personal growth and skill development at the same time, each individual taking from the cluster of skills and concepts involved the ones that he is ready to assimilate at the moment.

One method of getting a written extension of some of these activities, principally the smaller collages and the found poems, is to set up a kind of pen pal arrangement so that a student may actually mail his collage or found poem to another person outside the school or trade with a person from another class. These missives can be accompanied by some kind of letter either explaining the collage or giving some kind of description about the assignment. Pen pals might exchange *Self Collages* and then each write a brief character sketch to send back to the creator of the collage. Other possible audiences are the various shut-in groups—children's wards, convalescent hospitals, veterans' hospitals, or even prisoners in jail (We know of one highly successful letter-writing program between students and jail inmates). One more potential audience is public officials: For example, students might send their collages of a polluted or pollution-free America to members of Congress along with letters urging them to adopt strong resolutions to protect the environment.

These scissors and glue activities are useful techniques for fostering skill development and personal growth through action and directed reflection.

Chapter 6:

SOME USEFUL POETRY FORMS

Haiku, cinquains, shape poems, and the other forms listed below serve as useful vehicles for organizing and presenting material which has been previously generated by brainstorming, directed reflection, observation, or some other information-generating device. Because these forms are generally short and don't necessarily have to make logical sense, this kind of poetry writing often provides the ideal medium to help young people break the grip of writer's paralysis. As students work to distill the rich pool of raw material, they discover their own talents in the use of imagery, juxtaposition, emphasis, and other technical writing skills. Students find these writing experiences satisfying; they delight in their own successful creativity and the pleasure of hearing one another's work.

Robert Frost once described free verse as playing tennis with the net down. These forms are provided as nets, to make the job of shaping the poem more challenging so that the accomplishment is more highly valued. The forms also serve as discovery tools by providing limitations to work against.

None of the forms presented here requires a knowledge of scansion or rhyme schemes, such as those required for a sonnet or triolet, for example. There is no reason, however, that a teacher who wishes cannot use the more difficult forms in combination with brainstorming, etc.

HAIKU:

This is the hard-working Japanese form consisting of three lines—with five syllables in the first line, seven syllables in the second line, and five syllables in the last line. Often the last line serves to focus the other two by a juxtaposition of opposites, a concrete example, or a summing up of some kind. For example:

> *THE CHILD*
> *Changeable moods are*
> *Inquisitive—fragmented*
> *Creative motion.*

DOUBLE HAIKU:

Just as it says, this is a six-line poem of five, seven, five, five, seven, and five syllables per line. For example:

> *THE CHILD*
> *Bright pattern of life*
> *Never ending source of joy*
> *Change without notice*
> *Changing in motion*

Spinning, circling, fancy, fun
Unpredictable.

TANKA:

This is a haiku with two additional
seven-syllable lines at the end—five, seven,
five, seven, seven. Originally the tanka
was a challenge poem, with one person com-
posing the first three lines and then challenging another person to complete the
thought with the last two lines. Students
might work in pairs challenging each other
with tanka. An example:

> *THE CHILD*
> *Unexpected fun*
> *Forming beautiful patterns*
> *Fragile, bright, joyful*
> *Satisfying, shimmering*
> *A person can learn from one.*

CINQUAIN:

The cinquain is a five-line poem with
the following pattern:
One word (names the topic)
Two words (defines or describes the topic)
Three words (expresses action about the
    topic)
Four words (expresses an attitude about
    the topic)
One word (synonym for the topic).
    For example:

> *THE CHILD*
> *Child*
> *Young creation*

> Running, sleeping, growing
> A flower just budding
> Promise.

NAME POEM:

A variation of the word cinquain is the name poem:

> BETSEY
> Betsey
> Young elf
> Climbing, jumping, summersaulting
> She holds my heart
> Breathless.

Name poems should always be highly positive, focusing on strengths in the individual. As a positive focus activity, the class can make up name poems about each member. For this activity the class is divided into groups of four and then groups are paired. Each group of four then composes name poems about each of the members of the other group, brainstorming for ideas first. Then the two groups are joined, and each name poem is read.

SYLLABLE CINQUAIN:

The pattern of syllables for this five-line poem is two, four, six, eight, two:

> Snow comes
> A gentle mask
> Harsh on the face below
> Dashing the hope for early spring
> Softly.

SHAPE POEM:
    A poem can be written in the shape of
a tree, a cat, a sailboat, etc. Or it can
illustrate the story it tells, like this:

> *Threedaringtightropewalkers*
> *Thrilledtheexcitedcrowd*
> *Untilonefelloo_{f_f}*

PARALLEL POEMS AND THEME POEMS:[1]
    Parallel poems have the same basic
form with changes in the specific words:

> *I used to think . . .*
> *But now I know . . .*
> *I used to think . . .*
> *But now I know . . .*
>   (etc.)

    Theme poems follow a theme through the
poem, such as including a color in every
line or using a form such as the following:

> *Monday I . . .*
> *Tuesday I . . .*
>   *. . .*
> *Saturday I . . .*
> *But on Sunday I . . . .*

Numbers and the alphabet can also be used.

---

[1] *For a fuller treatment and examples
see Kenneth Koch,* Wishes, Lies, and Dreams:
Teaching Children to Write Poetry (*New York:
Random House, 1971).*

Chapter 7:

EXTENDED PROJECTS

SHORT STORIES:

Nearly everyone likes to read short stories. Many students clamor to be given a chance to write short stories, and most English teachers like the idea but are confronted by the problem of extent. A worthwhile short story is more than one night's worth of writing, yet to turn a class loose to "write a short story" for a week or more is, for many students at least, an invitation to procrastination and diffused and ineffective work. One solution is a structured series of assignments which build up elements which can then be synthesized into a complete short story.

The assignments outlined below are designed to produce a short story with a beginning, middle, and end, and with one (or more) well-rounded character(s). The total elapsed time from beginning to end must depend in part on how much else is going on in addition, but the story-writing process should never be rushed. Our customary spacing is one week for each of the first

three assignments and two weeks for the final
one. We always begin this project after
reading several short stories with Aristo-
telian structure, and as the writing proceeds, we continue reading stories and noting
techniques of characterization, creating
atmosphere, building suspense, and plotting
as we go. Desirable length for both the
preparatory assignments and the finished
story depend upon the maturity and linguis-
tic sophistication of the student.

Baldly stated, the component assignments are as follows:

Assignment #1: Write a character
sketch.

Assignment #2: Describe a place at a
particular time. Try to tell how it feels
to be there as well as what it looks like.

Assignment #3: Write an incident (NOT
a complete story) involving the character
you developed in Assignment #1.

Assignment #4: Write a complete short
story.

There is no reason to insist upon a
consistent thread of development from one
assignment to the next. False starts should
not be deprecated. Indeed, if the student
wishes to start fresh with Assignment #4,
that is his privilege. (In the context of
traditional grading, this policy can raise
the problem of plagiarism. We once inad-
vertently gave Isaac Asimov an A- for "The
Fun They Had.") But the judicious use of
brainstorming and allowing plenty of time
for conferences should solve most problems

in generating and handling material.

To get things started on a positive note of mutual support, it is a good idea to conduct a group brainstorming session before embarking on the first assignment. Brainstorm characters (real or fictitious) first, for one or two minutes at the most, and then select one to work on. Next, brainstorm for two minutes questions you would ask the character in order to get to know him or her. Then, with that list still visible, brainstorm for four or five minutes possible answers to those questions. If time allows, brainstorm also ways to get answers to the listed questions without asking the character. With all this information available students can then work in groups of three or four on developing a credible character from that material. Reports back to the class as a whole will undoubtedly show both considerable variety and ingenuity.

After the project is under way ample time should be provided in class for students to discuss their work with one another and with the teacher and for giving and receiving help when desired. One approach is to form support groups of three or four students each to stay together throughout the project. This way they get to know each other's needs and problems in some detail. Alternatively, small work groups can be formed fresh once a week or so for a single class period in which each member of the group presents a problem he needs or would like to have help with. With either arrangement, the group brainstorms possible solutions to each individual's problem, and each student can then go back to his own project with both an awareness of the needs of his fellow writers and a fresh bundle of ideas generated by the group.

Sample brainstorms by the whole class also continue to be helpful. For example, brainstorm for five minutes ways to describe what it's like to be adrift in a small boat in the fog off a rocky coast. In the event that all the senses are not touched upon in the course of the brainstorm, the teacher should bring those not included to the class's attention and extend the brainstorming period for another minute on those aspects.

Before final drafts are prepared the teacher should set aside a specific period of time (and extend it if necessary) for the giving and receiving of help with technical matters—items of form such as the paragraphing of dialogue and questions concerning style and the mechanics of expression.

When the great day comes, and everyone brings his completed story to class, as many as time allows should be shared immediately, with the rest following as soon as possible. When all who wish to have read their stories to the class, the stories should be collected into a loose-leaf anthology to be kept in an accessible place in the classroom. Ways of sharing with a wider audience include placing a copy of the anthology in the school library and, if time and technical resources permit, distributing mimeographed copies of some or all of the stories to students in other classes.

PAGES FOR AN AUTOBIOGRAPHY:
This is really a series of short assignments which can be collected into a telling autobiographical statement. Rather than organizing the autobiography on a time basis, *Pages for an Autobiography* uses a topical approach. Following are some possible topics:

What my dresser top says about me
My favorite relative
My longest journey
How I have spent my last five Saturday afternoons
An autobiography of my shoes
A hair autobiography
A skill that I am proud to have acquired

Once students get the idea, they can brainstorm their own topics. Then each student can select his own topics, and each autobiography can be constructed along individual lines.

In assigning *Pages for an Autobiography*, it is important that the teacher indicate whether the writing is to be public, for any to read, or private, for the student's eyes alone.

TAPED INTERVIEWS:

One little-used device for longer writings is the taped interview with an outside figure—the school principal, the mayor, the chief of police, a local writer, the baker, a local merchant, firefighter, etc.

In setting up the taped interview, it is important that the interviewer have a real interest in the subject and a genuine desire to know more about it. It may be necessary to do some research work before planning the actual interview. As with many of the other activities in this book, the research and planning may be fruitfully undertaken either by a small group or by an individual.

After settling on a figure to interview, setting up a time and place to conduct the interview, and doing any basic research, the students should brainstorm specific questions and then select those that seem potentially most productive. The teacher may wish to conduct a short lesson on question-asking at this point in order to help students to develop questions which will call for more than one-word answers, or which will follow specific trains of thought.

It may be appropriate to conduct a role-played interview as a rehearsal.

For the interview itself, it is generally best to set and keep a specific length of time, such as fifteen minutes. If the interview is to be conducted by a group, it is usually more effective for a single spokesman to do the questioning.

The play-back of the tape, of course, can serve as a presentation of the information. However, for a more finished work, one which might be included in the student newspaper or magazine, a transcript can be prepared and edited to reduce repetition and give focus and emphasis to the finished work. When any substantial editing is done, it is good practice to submit the edited transcript to the person interviewed for review and comment.

A variation of the *Taped Interview* is the "man-on-the-street" interview. Here the objective is to get a variety of opinions on a given topic from varied sources. Here planning and shaping the questions is again important, although generally each interview will be limited to one or two questions. Once again the tape can stand on its own, or editions can be made to present a more comprehensive view of the interviews.

As an elaboration of the "man-on-the-street" interview, the interviewer might take a picture of each interviewee. (This is a good place for a Polaroid camera.) The pictures can be displayed with the answers, or as a test of empathy, four pictures might be posted along with four statements, and then other members of the class might guess which statement goes with which picture.

PLAYS:

W. Denis Johnston, the Irish playwright, has pointed out that most fiction can be classified into seven basic plots: (1) The Cinderella plot, where unrecognized virtue is recognized (often by a gimmick such as a glass slipper). (2) The Persephone plot, where a gift is taken away, and the hero struggles to regain with gift (with or without success). (3) The Oedipus, or fatal flaw plot, where the audience sees the workings of fate. (4) The questing plot, where the hero is in search of something (he may or may not ever find it). (5) The Faust plot, or the debt that must be paid. (6) The Hamlet plot, or the wrong to be righted. And (7) the eternal triangle plot.

Johnston suggests that any one of these plots can be used to make a good play, but that the playwright should avoid using a combination of two or more of these plots in any one play.

For this activity, the teacher may wish to choose one or two or three of the plots and explain each to the class. Then the class is divided into groups of four or five, and each group chooses a plot and brainstorms specifics of that plot (e.g. What is the gift that is taken away? What is the wrong to be righted? By whom? How?)

Each group then works out a playlet of five minutes or so which can be presented to the class on the following day.

If any group wishes, they can continue to work out details and write a more extensive script. Following adequate rehearsal, this play can then be presented to the class as a whole or to a larger audience.

STORIES FOR YOUNGER CHILDREN:
This is a project which involves upper grade students working with younger ones, eighth graders with first graders, for instance. The older student helps the younger one to invent a story, perhaps using informal brainstorming or a forced fit (*"What about a story with a king and an orange and an alligator?"*).

The two students then collaborate to make a booklet of the story, with the younger student supplying the pictures, the older one writing the words.

GROUP RESEARCH PAPER:
In situations where it seems advisable or necessary to teach research writing, the *Group Research Paper* can provide a useful introduction. The topic is organized and researched by the group, and then the work is divided among the individuals for the final write-up.

To get started, the class divides itself into groups of two to five along lines of interest or compatibility. Next, each group brainstorms broad interest areas and then chooses one to pursue. The group then brainstorms topics from the broad area that they have chosen, finally picking one topic to pursue further. If the topic is still too broad, the group can brainstorm subtopics and choose one. The important thing is to narrow the field through brainstorming and choosing so that the final topic chosen is one that can be covered adequately within the scope of the paper.

At this point the group is ready to begin its research. The group can brainstorm possible resources of information, and the teacher can often supply others. Then the group divides the resources among themselves and digs into the material, taking notes on index cards. (Here a short lesson on note-taking may be useful, as well as advice concerning bibliographical references.)

The group re-assembles and immediately brainstorms sub-divisions for their topic. This list of sub-divisions will suggest one and perhaps several ways of organizing the paper. The group then chooses one method of organization and divides the list of organized sections among the group members. Each member then uses this organization scheme to sort his index cards, giving each pile to the member who has been assigned that section. Index cards that don't fit the organization are thrown into a "miscellaneous" category which can be written up into a section or not, as the group chooses.

The writing is done by individuals from the cards and from their general knowledge of the topic. Each section is then read by at least two other members of the group, who make suggestions about matters of style and content. The pieces are then fitted together to form the finished product.

As with other public writing, these group research papers should be shared within the class and with interested audiences outside the classroom if possible.

III:

FURTHER CONSIDERATIONS

Chapter 8:

MECHANICS

The problem of what to do about mechanics in teaching composition is just that—a problem. The needs of the student run counter to the felt needs of the adults around him: His teachers want papers that are neatly written, properly spelled, and grammatically correct, and therefore easy to read. His parents want him to be able to write thank-you notes to Granny and Aunt Sarah that will be impressive, and that means neatly written, properly spelled and punctuated, and grammatically correct—the content of a conventional thank-you note is of virtually no consequence. The student, on the other hand, doesn't want to put any real effort into writing unless he has something which he considers important to say to someone whom he hopes to influence in some way. And his judgment of the correctness and effectiveness of his writing is purely utilitarian: If the message gets across, the medium is satisfactory.

Perhaps the worst enemy of increasing the effectiveness of a student's writing is grading. Whatever the particular basis of grading, it is a cruelly paradoxical business to ask a student to stretch himself, to try something more difficult than he has done before, and then mark him down for faltering rather than praising him for making the attempt. Furthermore, no matter who the stated audience may be, if a paper is to be graded, the real audience in the writer's mind is the grader, because it is the grader who must be influenced.

The same principle applies to the marking of mechanical errors on a paper, even without assigning a grade. Unless specifically requested by the student, marking mechanical errors is counterproductive: The student sees himself being judged against an unattainable standard of perfection, and in order to avoid seeing his paper, as one student of ours put it, "bleeding to death" with red marks, he retreats to the safety of familiar, easily spelled vocabulary and simple sentence patterns. This, of course, makes the teaching of composition an exercise in futility.

The student who has something important to say will concern himself with the effectiveness of his communication. If his audience fails to understand his message because of faulty organization, erratic spelling or punctuation, or awkward style, he will be intensely interested in correcting those difficulties. It is at this point, and not before, that the mechanics of expressions should be taken up—at the request of the writer.

If at all possible, instruction in mechanics should be done on an individualized basis, so that each student gets what he needs when he needs it. This is not always possible, of course, and often there seems to be an epidemic of a particular type of error. In such cases the whole class or a small group can work together, but the objects of study should be the student writing involved, not drill sentences out of a book.

One of the best techniques we have found for dealing with mechanics is to set aside a specific (and elastic) period of time for answering questions on mechanics and style just before the end of a writing project. Thus the student can try new sentence structures, stretch his vocabulary or use of imagery, or whatever, and if he is unsure about his success, he can show it to his teacher and get expert advice and a chance to revise *before* his work goes on public display. This consultation time is especially important in a situation where student compositions are given grades, for it offers an exemption from failure due to experimentation and and thus allows the student to stretch himself with a measure of safety.

In connection with work periods of this sort it is important to remember that students can be valuable resources for each other. Students can work in small groups, helping each other as much as they can and then referring more difficult problems to the teacher. Students from one class can work with younger students, either on a one-to-one basis or in small groups. Or students can simply consult one another on an informal basis. Since there is a wide range of skill levels in even the most homogeneous of groupings, this kind of cooperative work enhances the learning opportunities of the weaker students and helps the more advanced to codify their knowledge (the best way to learn anything is to teach it).

Chapter 9:

COORDINATING

WRITING WITH LITERATURE

Various reasons are offered for the
teaching of English and American literature to junior and senior high school students, but they generally center on the
notions of transmitting the valuable por-
tions of our cultural heritage, helping
students to develop their critical thinking skills, and encouraging them to read
"good" literature for pleasure. Often the
materials and techniques chosen to achieve
the first two aims work against the last,
but this need not necessarily be the case.

An individual's reasons for liking
any particular work of literature—poem,
play, story, novel, essay—are largely
personal. One can appreciate a work for
its historical or cultural importance and
therefore hold it dear, but that is a different, generally more intellectual and
less emotional, matter. One likes a work
which carries with it positive personal
associations: I like this play because

I enjoyed acting in it. I like that poem
because it was read to me often when I was
a small child. I like this one because
I've always had success teaching it. And
so on. One also likes works to which one
can respond empathetically, works which
shed light on some aspect of one's own experience, which help crystallize one's
thoughts—works in which the reader recog-
nizes some element of himself or his situation.

It is the task of the English teacher
to so structure his students' experiences
with literature that they will have both
pleasant personal associations with the
things they read and opportunities to respond to their reading empathetically.
Obviously part of this task lies in the
selection of the literature to be read,
but there is also much that can be done
through classroom activities, both oral
and written.

For many works of literature, especially those which stand at some distance
in time and/or space from the students, the
introduction of the work is all-important.
There are two basic types of experience
which will help the student to respond to
the new work in a positive manner—experiences which parallel that of the author
in writing the work, and experiences which
parallel that which may have provided the
author's impulse to write a particular
work. Often these can be combined.

For example, before introducing

Robert Frost's "The Road Not Taken," the teacher might ask the class to brainstorm major decisions that a teenager like themselves might have to make in the next one, two, or five years. With the brainstormed list of decisions to draw from, the class is divided into small groups. Each group then chooses one of the decision areas to work on and brainstorms possible consequences. After each group has reported back to the whole class, each student chooses one decision and writes a paragraph, speaking as a person who has made or is about to make that decision. Paragraphs can be shared either in small groups or with the class as a whole.

Another approach to the same poem is to have the class brainstorm images for a dilemma. Small groups then choose one image and develop supporting details. At this point each group can write a collective paragraph or poem, or the groups can report back to the class as a whole. Then each individual writes briefly on whatever image he wishes. Again, papers can be shared in small groups or with the whole class and can be posted on a bulletin board. The same procedure can be followed using examples of a dilemma rather than images.

A useful activity to help bridge the gap between the abstraction of theme and the concreteness of image and action is the following: The abstraction—courage, kindness, honor, . . .—is written at the top of the center of the blackboard. On

the left side is the word *is*, to the right,
is not. The class brainstorms instances
and examples for each category. This can
be done in turn, *is*'s first, then *is not*'s,
or simultaneously, since positive illustrations almost inevitably lead one to
think of opposites. And there are many
instances that will fit into both cate-
gories (e.g. *Kindness is/is not doing something for someone that he could have done
for himself.*).

The brainstorming can be followed by
writing of paragraphs or short poems either
individually or in small groups. Or this
material can be used for a more extended
writing assignment. Doing this activity
on courage prior to reading Stephen Crane's
The Red Badge of Courage, for example,
sharpens the student's awareness and helps
bridge the cultural gap between the Civil
War and the post-Vietnam era.

A more direct way of involving students in the author's process of composition is to let them actually write a portion
of the work under study. This can be done
at any point in the course of reading the
work. In advance, the teacher can present
a brief scenario and ask each member of the
class to write a detailed sketch of one of
the characters involved, which can then be
checked against the author's perceptions.

During the course of reading the work,
this type of activity can take a number of
forms. Having read up to a critical con-
frontation, students can be asked to write

the ensuing scene before reading the author's version. Or having read the first half or so of a short story, the class, again either individually or in small groups, can finish the story. Once the class has read enough of a play or novel to be fairly well acquainted with the major characters, students can write up imaginary interviews with characters of their own choosing or conversations between a chosen character and someone else in the student's own world.

In all of these activities the sharing of writings and the discussion among the students of their differing perceptions and modes of expression are important ingredients in the learning process. This sharing enriches the insights that the individual gains by viewing his own perceptions and writings in relation to those of the author.

After a work of fiction or drama has been read, creative writing assignments linked to the literature can provide both pleasant personal involvement for the student and important evaluative information for the teacher. The student who writes an intervening incident to be inserted at a specified point in the work just read has a chance to exercise his imagination, perhaps enlarging on something he feels the author slighted or developing totally new compatible material. At the same time he demonstrates by his treatment of his own material his understanding of the literature, especially in the area of characterization.

Another activity, useful during or
after reading a novel or play, is to ask
the members of the class to rank order the
principal characters, from the one they
like most to the one they like least, and
then write one paragraph justifying the
number one ranking and one paragraph justifying the bottom ranking. These rank-
orders and supporting paragraphs should
be shared in small groups. As an extension, each group can be asked to arrive at
a consensus ranking and present a written
report to the rest of the class.

Another writing activity which provides an alternative to analytical papers
and allows intuitive but unarticulated insights to be revealed is to write something
which is in some way (It is best to specify
only one way.) like the work just read.   For
example, after reading Robert Frost's
"Stopping by Woods on a Snowy Evening"
write a short poem about woods, or about
snow.   Or write a poem about stopping to
look at something you pass nearly every
day.   Or write a poem about anything you
like, using the same form as "Stopping by
Woods."   In many circumstances it is helpful for the class or small groups to brainstorm potential raw materials or supporting
details.   It is important to restrict the
writing in only one way—subject, form,
theme, etc.—in order to allow a maximum
of freedom of choice for the student writer.
(In this regard it is generally wise to re-

fuse to answer questions asking for more details about how to do the activity. The answer to all such questions is, "That's up to you to decide.") As with the other writing activities included here, sharing the results with the class is an important part of the activity.

Our favorite example of the success of this last activity occurred in a ninth grade class which had just finished reading Burton Raffel's translation of *Beowulf*. We asked the students to write monster stories. The resulting stories ranged from hitherto-unknown incidents in the lives of Beowulf and Grendel (both separately and together) through medieval dragons and Halloween tales to futuristic science fiction and present-day UFO's. The most revealing of these tales, and one of the class's favorites, was an additional encounter between the young Beowulf and a sea-monster written by a student whose words and implied attitudes during preceding class discussions had indicated that if, indeed, he was reading the poem, he was getting very little out of it. His story, however, revealed through its style and selection of detail that he had, in fact, not only read *Beowulf* but also thoroughly absorbed its atmosphere and rhetorical techniques.

Chapter 10:

EVALUATION

Although the authors of this book strongly disapprove of the grading systems traditionally used in American schools, we feel that evaluation of the procedures and the product of the educational process is both necessary and desirable. Teachers need information on the effectiveness of the various aspects of their work and the impact it has on their students. Students, in turn, need the opportunity to reflect upon what they have been doing and to communicate their needs and desires to teachers, fellow students, and anyone else in a position to influence the future course of their education.

The suggestions which follow are based upon the principles of maximizing communication among those involved in the teaching-learning process, which we view as a cooperative endeavor, and of generating feedback, as much as possible, on an on-going basis, rather than waiting for the completion of a unit of work.

STUDENT FEEDBACK:

Feedback from students takes many forms, from slouching postures or alert, bright eyes to formal documents. The *Student Feedback Form* (see page 101) is one type of formalized feedback. This form is designed to be used once a week (preferably on the same day each week). Ten minutes or so of class time should be allowed for the completion of the form, and the teacher should comment on the information thus received at the next class meeting, noting any generally prevailing opinions and dissenting ones and stating the possibilities for carrying out suggested changes. A less formal means of collecting written feedback is maintaining a *Feedback Box.*[1]

TEACHER SELF-EVALUATION:

Teachers are very busy people. Often we think, "Wouldn't it be nice to be able to sit down and just think about what I'm doing and why," but we don't take the time. We should. Reflecting on the events of a class, especially if done immediately following the class, is a valuable method of self-evaluation for both students and teachers. The *Teacher Self-Evaluation Form* (see page 104) provides a framework within which

---

[1] *For further details on this and other suggestions for generating student feedback, see Robert C. Hawley & Isabel L. Hawley,* A Handbook of Personal Growth Activities for Classroom Use *(Amherst, Mass.: E R A Press, 1972), pp. 37-42.*

to reflect upon a just-completed class.
It can be duplicated and used in a formal
way, modified to meet the specific needs
of the teacher, or simply used as a guide
to indicate directions in which to probe.
The important thing is for the teacher to
make a habit of reviewing and evaluating
classroom procedures and making notes
about outstanding successes and possible
improvements while the events of the class
are still fresh in his or her mind.

STUDENT SELF-EVALUATION:

If a concrete, qualitative measure of
achievement is desirable to meet the needs
of an individual student or necessary in
order to fulfill the requirements of the
educational establishment, one possible
approach is to use a *Student Self-Evaluation Form.* The format should be tailored
to the needs of the particular situation.
The evaluation can be done either by the
student alone or by the student and teacher *together* in conference. The sample
form included here (see pages 102-103)
was developed by Liz Freeman and Phil
Rouvales for use in their English and
social studies classes at Pollard Junior
High School in Needham, Massachusetts.

INDIVIDUALIZED CONTRACTS:

Individual project contracts, either
between student and teacher or by the student with himself, offer a structure for
individualizing activity in the classroom,

and they can, if necessary, provide a framework for evaluation which can be turned into a grade. Whatever its purpose, each contract should be written and should include the following: student's name; name of sponsor (teacher or other resource person); brief descriptive title; a brief statement of objective(s); planned activities; projected completion time; criteria for evaluation; (and, if necessary, criteria for grading). The contract should be signed by the individual(s) involved, and it should be open to re-negotiation whenever the need arises.

UNOBTRUSIVE MEANS OF EVALUATION:
     All good teachers are conscious of and respond to a variety of unobtrusive measures of the success of current classroom activities—inattention manifested by vacant stares at the ceiling or out the window or by irrelevant conversation; animated and enthusiastic discussion of the subject at hand; eager asking of questions; puzzled looks not followed by questions; etc. Such measures are exceedingly valuable both for their timeliness and for their unobtrusiveness.
     Broad observations of this nature are particularly helpful in determining when to end an activity or introduce a new element or approach. They can also be used as measures of the success of student writing. The general noise level in the classroom as a student is reading his story aloud,

for instance, is inversely proportional to the involvement of the audience with the reading. Another such measure of the general success of student writing is the wear and tear on pages in the loose-leaf class anthology.

Similarly, unobtrusive observation of changes in the behavior of a particular student can be quite valuable in assessing progress and analyzing needs. Perceptible relaxation by an initially tense student or increased contribution to brainstorms and discussions by a reticent youngster, for example, indicates increased self-confidence in the classroom situation. Very often, increased length of student compositions is an indication of an enhanced ease of expression. Conversely, a student whose writing is initially rambling and verbose will tend to say more in less space as he sharpens his skills in organization and expression.

Unobtrusive evaluation of this sort is by its nature somewhat imprecise. Nevertheless, a thoughtfully collected anecdotal record of such observations, coupled with examples of the student's work, is a far more significant measure of a student's accomplishments than is an alphabetical or numerical distillation.

STUDENT FEEDBACK FORM

1. How satisfied were you with this week's sessions? (Circle one.)

1   2   3   4   5   6   7
very   very
dissatisfied   satisfied

2. What was the high point of your week in class?

3. What factors contributed towards your satisfaction?

4. What could be changed to make these sessions better for you?

5. What can I do to make these sessions better for you?

6. What can you do for yourself to make these sessions better for you?

7. What are some of the special issues, concerns, or questions that you would like to see raised in class next week?

8. Free comment/suggestions/questions/jokes/etc.:

_____
Name *(optional)*

STUDENT SELF-EVALUATION FORM

Name:
Date:

Subject:
Teacher:

QUALITY OF WORK RELATIVE TO CLASS
*My work, relative to the rest of
the class, is:*

Excellent	25 pts.
Above average	22 pts.
Average	19 pts.
Below average	13 pts.
QUALITY POINTS	_____

QUALITY OF WORK RELATIVE TO
   PRESENT ABILITY
I work to the best of my ability:

All the time	25 pts.
Most of the time	21 pts.
Some of the time	17 pts.
Rarely	13 pts.
QUALITY POINTS	_____

EFFORT IN WORK
I try hard:

All of the time	25 pts.
Most of the time	21 pts.
Some of the time	17 pts.
Rarely	13 pts.
EFFORT POINTS	_____

PRIDE IN WORK (Self-evaluation
   only)
I feel proud of my work:

Always	5 pts.
Sometimes	3 pts.
Rarely	1 pt.
Never	0 pts.
PRIDE POINTS	_____

COMMUNICATION IN THE CLASSROOM

The following behavior is:

	Typical of me (5 pts.)	Not typical of me (0 pts.)
I listen when the teacher speaks.	_____	_____
I listen when other students speak.	_____	_____
I ask questions when I don't understand.	_____	_____
I contribute to class discussions.	_____	_____
COMMUNICATION POINTS	_____	

ADDITIONAL COMMENTS
(Student or teacher)

EXTRA CREDIT
Criteria:

Points _____

TOTAL POINTS _____

PARENTS' COMMENTS *(and signature)*

1.   Did the members of the class seem to understand my objectives?

2.   Was I able to elicit objectives from the members of the class and incorporate them into the lesson?

3.   Circle one number on each of the following continuums to indicate an overall impression of the classroom behavior:

a. 1   2   3   4   5   6   7
   purposeful   frivolous

b. 1   2   3   4   5   6   7
   spirited   solemn

c. 1   2   3   4   5   6   7
   friendly   hostile

4.   Jot down a sentence or two about what you felt were the best features of the class.

5.   What would you like to change before doing it again?

6.   Open comment:

Chapter 11:

ADDITIONAL RESOURCES

Brown, Rosellen, et al. *The Whole Word Catalogue*. New York: Teachers and Writers Collaborative Inc., 1972. A special issue of the *Teachers and Writers Collaborative Newsletter* (Volume 4, Number 3, Summer 1972), this is a valuable collection of writing activities together with examples of student writing. Also contains sections on materials, resources, and helpful books and magazines.

Hawley, Robert C., and Isabel L. Hawley. *A Handbook of Personal Growth Activities for Classroom Use*. Amherst, Mass.: ERA Press, 1972. Contains many activities which can stimulate written expression as well as suggestions for their use in the classroom.

Hawley, Robert C. *Human Values in the Classroom: Teaching for Personal and Social Growth*. Amherst, Mass.: ERA Press, 1973. A conceptual framework for approaching teaching as a means for promoting the personal and social growth of each student.

Details a sequence of teaching concerns
which provide a structure for teachers who
wish to implement the approach.

Koch, Kenneth. *Wishes, Lies, and
Dreams: Teaching Children to Write Poetry*.
New York: Random House, 1971. An account
of the approach that Koch uses in teaching
poetry writing to New York City elementary
school students, including specific activities and examples of student writing. Although Koch works mostly with the younger
elementary grades, these activities can be
easily adapted for use with older children.

Moffett, James. *A Student-Centered
Language Arts Curriculum, Grades K-13: A
Handbook for Teachers*. Boston: Houghton
Mifflin Company, 1968. Practical suggestions for revamping and opening up the
language arts curriculum. Includes many
specific activities for classroom use.

Moffett, James. *Teaching the Universe
of Discourse*. Boston: Houghton-Mifflin
Company, 1968. Sets a theoretical framework for the student-activity-centered
approach to developing skills in language.

Simon, Sidney B., Robert C. Hawley, and
David D. Britton. *Composition for Personal
Growth: Values Clarification Through Writ-
ing*. New York: Hart Publishing Co., 1973.
An approach to teaching written composition
through personal growth and value clarify-

ing activities. Proceeds from the assumption that writing is a means to achieve reflection, clarification, and commitment in one's personal life. Abounds with specific activities and suggestions for their use in the classroom.

Additions:

INDEX OF ACTIVITIES